OXFORD MUSIC FOR ORGAN

GERRE HANCOCK
AIR
A Prelude for Organ

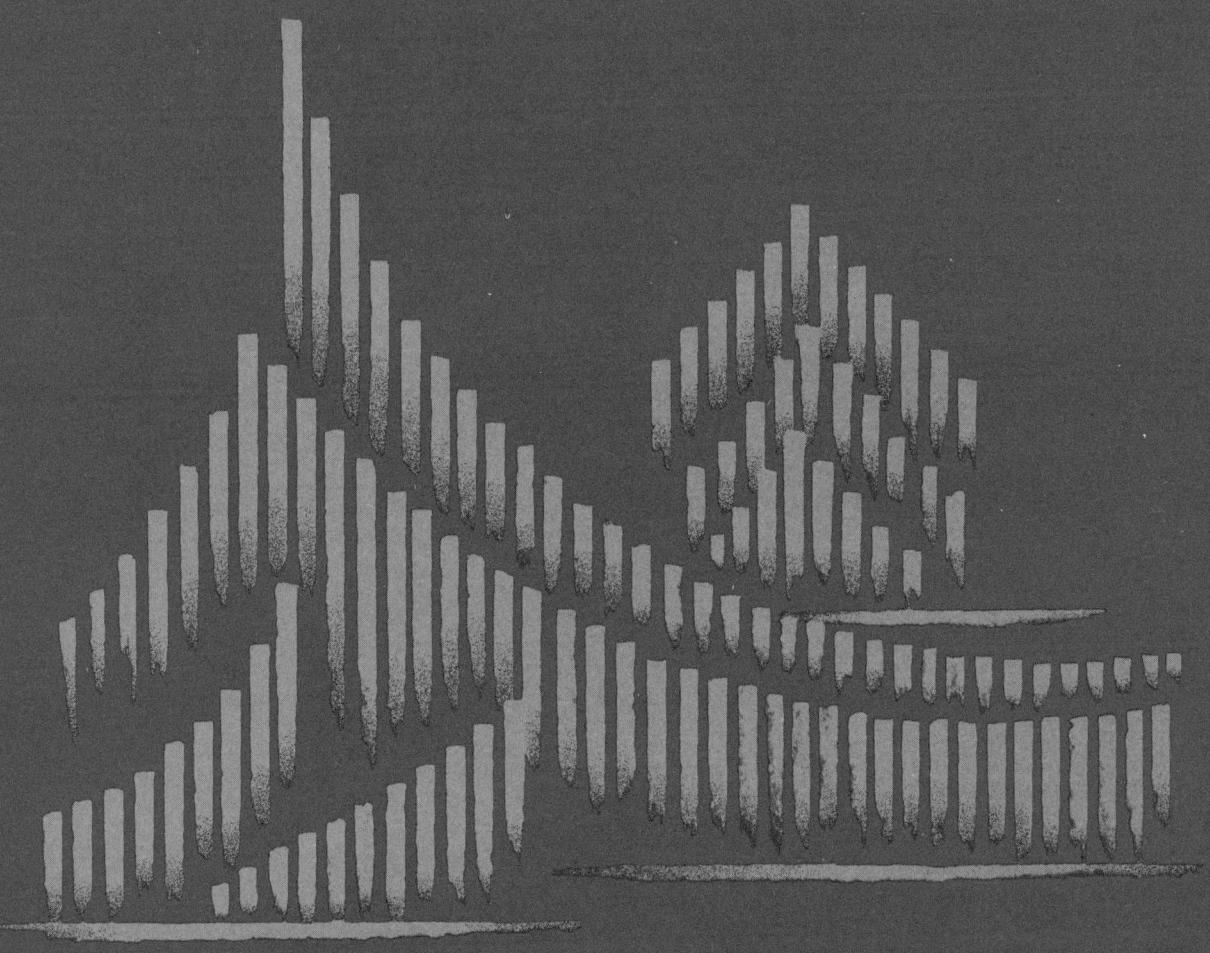

OXFORD
UNIVERSITY PRESS

Gerre Hancock (b. 1934, Lubbock, Texas) is Organist and Master of the Choristers at St. Thomas Church in New York City. He has received music degrees from the University of Texas and from Union Theological Seminary in New York and has studied organ with E. William Doty, Robert Baker, Jean Langlais, and Marie-Claire Alain and improvisation with Nadia Boulanger and M. Searle Wright.

A Fellow of the American Guild of Organists, he was a member of its National Council and is a founder and past President of the Association of Anglican Musicians. He currently serves on the faculties of the Juilliard School in New York City and the Institute of Sacred Music at Yale University and on a visiting basis at the Eastman School of Music.

Hancock has performed in cities throughout the United States and abroad and has been a featured recitalist at regional and national conventions of the American Guild of Organists. He is an imaginative service player and an extraordinary improviser. His expertise and many years' teaching experience have been codified in *Improvising: How to Master the Art* (OUP, 1994).

for Judy

AIR

A Prelude for Organ

Sw. Solo Stop 8'
Gt. Foundation Stops 8', 4' (*f*)
Ch. Flutes 8', 4'
Ped. Soft 16', 8', Ch. to Ped.

Gerre Hancock

Copyright © 2000, Oxford University Press, Inc.

Printed in U.S.A.

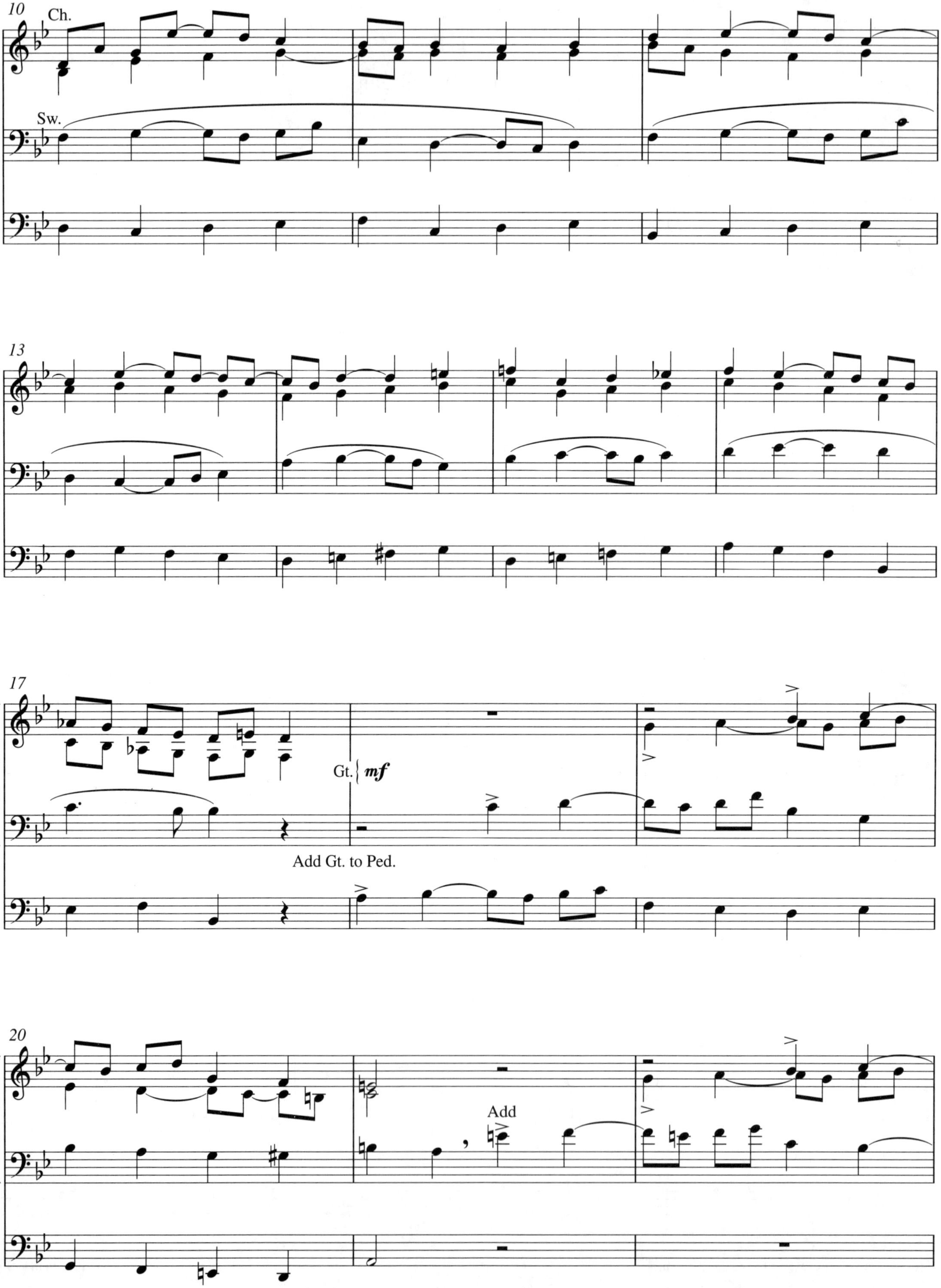
10
Ch.
Sw.
13
17
Gt. mf
Add Gt. to Ped.
20
Add

–November, 1960
New York, NY

The Music of Gerre Hancock
Available from Oxford University Press

A Paraphrase on "St. Elizabeth"	organ	0-19-385754-5
Christ Our Passover	SATB, congregation, trumpets, trombones, organ	
	—Choral score (with cong. part)	0-19-386173-9
	—Full score and set of parts	0-19-386174-7
Come, Ye Lofty, Come, Ye Lowly	youth/children's choirs, SATB, organ	0-19-386053-8
Communion Service ("Missa Resurrectionis")	SATB, organ	0-19-385563-1
Eternal God	SATB, organ	0-19-385912-2
Improvising: How to Master the Art	textbook for organ	0-19-385881-9
Infant Holy, Infant Lowly	SATB, organ	0-19-386224-7
Judge Eternal	SATB, organ	0-19-385802-9
Kindle the Gift of God	SATB, organ	0-19-386216-6
A Meditation on "Draw Us in the Spirit's Tether"	organ	0-19-386052-X
O Be Joyful in the Lord	youth choir, SATB, organ	0-19-385964-5
O King Enthroned on High	SATB, organ	0-19-386055-4
O Lord, Our Governor	SATB, organ	0-19-386054-6
A Song to the Lamb	SATB, brass, timpani, organ	0-19-386255-7
	Set of brass and timpani parts	0-19-386256-5
The Lord Will Surely Come	SATB, organ	0-19-385913-0

OXFORD
UNIVERSITY PRESS

www.oup.com

ISBN 0-19-386271-9

9 780193 862715

Cat. No. 93.104   Price $8.95